Hop, Skip and Jump

Julie Ellis

OXFORD
UNIVERSITY PRESS

I like to hop. Can you hop?

I like to skip. Can you skip?

I like to jump. Can you jump?

We like to run. Can you run?

We like to crawl.
Can you crawl?

We like to roll.
Can you roll?

We like to play with
Mum and Dad.